# The British Museum

## DIARY 2018

FRANCES
LINCOLN

First published in 2017 by Frances Lincoln, an imprint of
The Quarto Group. www.QuartoKnows.com

A catalogue record for this book is available from
the British Library

978-0-7112-3865-7

Printed and bound in China

9 8 7 6 5 4 3 2 1

Title page: Pectoral in the form of a 'wedjat'-eye,
Third Intermediate Period, 1069–945 BC, Egypt,
British Museum EA26300

This page: Netsuke showing a group of foxes, Edo
period, 18th–19th century, Japan, British Museum
1945,1017.521, bequeathed by Oscar Charles Raphael

Cover, left to right, top to bottom: Tin-glazed
earthenware plate, c.1520–70, Umbria, The Marches,
Italy, British Museum 1851,1201.21; Porcelain
plate, 1921, made at the State Porcelain Factory,
St Petersburg, the decoration designed and painted
by Natalya Girschfeld, Russia, British Museum
1990,0506.3; Silver plate, Roman, 200–270, found at
Chaource, France, British Museum 1890,0923.1; Tin-
glazed, lustred earthenware plate, c.1525–30, workshop
of Giorgio Andreoli, Gubbio, Italy, British Museum
1878,1230.391; Painted pottery dish, 16th century,
Iznik, Turkey, British Museum Godman Colelction 42;
Tin-glazed, lustred earthenware plate, c.1688–1710,
painted by Siro Antonio Africa and Siro Domenico
Africa, workshop of Carlo Giuseppe Rampini, Pavia,
Italy, British Museum 1855,0313.15; Porcelain dish
decorated in wucai style, Ming dynasty, c.1522–66,
Jingdezhen, China, British Museum Sir Percival
David Collection, A.731, on loan from the Sir Percival
David Foundation of Chinese Art; Brown lustre plate,
tin-glazed, earthenware plate, c.1500–25, workshop
of Giorgio Andreoli, Gubbio, Italy, British Museum
1855,0313.5; Tin-glazed earthenware plate, c.1894–97,
Deruta, Italy, British Museum 1898,0523.15; Tin-
glazed earthenware plate, c.1490–1520, Umbria,
Orvieto, Italy, British Museum 1898,0523.14; Tin-
glazed earthenware plate, 1534, workshop of Piero
Bergantini, Faenza, Italy, British Museum 1891,0325.1;
Tin-glazed ceramic plate, c.1630–40, made by Denis
Lefebvre, Nevers, France, British Museum 2008,8002.1;
Tin-glazed earthenware plate, 1537, Urbino, Italy,
British Museum 1878,1230.429; Painted, glazed pottery
dish, 16th century, Iznik, Turkey, British Museum
Godman Collection 138; Tin-glazed earthenware
plate, c.1560–80, Montelupo Fiorentino, Italy, British
Museum 1899,0508.53; Painted pottery plate, East
Greek, c.620–600 BC, Miletus, Kamiros, Greece, British
Museum 1860,0201.12; Earthenware plate, 16th
century, Tuscany, Italy, British Museum 1878,1230.420;
Nabeshima ware dish, 1720s–40s, Edo period, Hizen,
Japan, British Museum Franks Collection 1283.+,
donated by Sir Augustus Wollaston Franks; Tin-glazed
earthenware plate, c.1535–50, Faenza, Italy, British
Museum 1878,1230.454; Tin-glazed earthenware plate,
1711, painted by James Thornhill, Delft, Netherlands,
British Museum 1889,0706.71

# CALENDAR 2018

### JANUARY
| M | T | W | T | F | S | S |
|---|---|---|---|---|---|---|
| 1 | 2 | 3 | 4 | 5 | 6 | 7 |
| 8 | 9 | 10 | 11 | 12 | 13 | 14 |
| 15 | 16 | 17 | 18 | 19 | 20 | 21 |
| 22 | 23 | 24 | 25 | 26 | 27 | 28 |
| 29 | 30 | 31 | | | | |

### FEBRUARY
| M | T | W | T | F | S | S |
|---|---|---|---|---|---|---|
| | | | 1 | 2 | 3 | 4 |
| 5 | 6 | 7 | 8 | 9 | 10 | 11 |
| 12 | 13 | 14 | 15 | 16 | 17 | 18 |
| 19 | 20 | 21 | 22 | 23 | 24 | 25 |
| 26 | 27 | 28 | | | | |

### MARCH
| M | T | W | T | F | S | S |
|---|---|---|---|---|---|---|
| | | | 1 | 2 | 3 | 4 |
| 5 | 6 | 7 | 8 | 9 | 10 | 11 |
| 12 | 13 | 14 | 15 | 16 | 17 | 18 |
| 19 | 20 | 21 | 22 | 23 | 24 | 25 |
| 26 | 27 | 28 | 29 | 30 | 31 | |

### APRIL
| M | T | W | T | F | S | S |
|---|---|---|---|---|---|---|
| | | | | | | 1 |
| 2 | 3 | 4 | 5 | 6 | 7 | 8 |
| 9 | 10 | 11 | 12 | 13 | 14 | 15 |
| 16 | 17 | 18 | 19 | 20 | 21 | 22 |
| 23 | 24 | 25 | 26 | 27 | 28 | 29 |
| 30 | | | | | | |

### MAY
| M | T | W | T | F | S | S |
|---|---|---|---|---|---|---|
| | 1 | 2 | 3 | 4 | 5 | 6 |
| 7 | 8 | 9 | 10 | 11 | 12 | 13 |
| 14 | 15 | 16 | 17 | 18 | 19 | 20 |
| 21 | 22 | 23 | 24 | 25 | 26 | 27 |
| 28 | 29 | 30 | 31 | | | |

### JUNE
| M | T | W | T | F | S | S |
|---|---|---|---|---|---|---|
| | | | | 1 | 2 | 3 |
| 4 | 5 | 6 | 7 | 8 | 9 | 10 |
| 11 | 12 | 13 | 14 | 15 | 16 | 17 |
| 18 | 19 | 20 | 21 | 22 | 23 | 24 |
| 25 | 26 | 27 | 28 | 29 | 30 | |

### JULY
| M | T | W | T | F | S | S |
|---|---|---|---|---|---|---|
| | | | | | | 1 |
| 2 | 3 | 4 | 5 | 6 | 7 | 8 |
| 9 | 10 | 11 | 12 | 13 | 14 | 15 |
| 16 | 17 | 18 | 19 | 20 | 21 | 22 |
| 23 | 24 | 25 | 26 | 27 | 28 | 29 |
| 30 | 31 | | | | | |

### AUGUST
| M | T | W | T | F | S | S |
|---|---|---|---|---|---|---|
| | | 1 | 2 | 3 | 4 | 5 |
| 6 | 7 | 8 | 9 | 10 | 11 | 12 |
| 13 | 14 | 15 | 16 | 17 | 18 | 19 |
| 20 | 21 | 22 | 23 | 24 | 25 | 26 |
| 27 | 28 | 29 | 30 | 31 | | |

### SEPTEMBER
| M | T | W | T | F | S | S |
|---|---|---|---|---|---|---|
| | | | | | 1 | 2 |
| 3 | 4 | 5 | 6 | 7 | 8 | 9 |
| 10 | 11 | 12 | 13 | 14 | 15 | 16 |
| 17 | 18 | 19 | 20 | 21 | 22 | 23 |
| 24 | 25 | 26 | 27 | 28 | 29 | 30 |

### OCTOBER
| M | T | W | T | F | S | S |
|---|---|---|---|---|---|---|
| 1 | 2 | 3 | 4 | 5 | 6 | 7 |
| 8 | 9 | 10 | 11 | 12 | 13 | 14 |
| 15 | 16 | 17 | 18 | 19 | 20 | 21 |
| 22 | 23 | 24 | 25 | 26 | 27 | 28 |
| 29 | 30 | 31 | | | | |

### NOVEMBER
| M | T | W | T | F | S | S |
|---|---|---|---|---|---|---|
| | | | 1 | 2 | 3 | 4 |
| 5 | 6 | 7 | 8 | 9 | 10 | 11 |
| 12 | 13 | 14 | 15 | 16 | 17 | 18 |
| 19 | 20 | 21 | 22 | 23 | 24 | 25 |
| 26 | 27 | 28 | 29 | 30 | | |

### DECEMBER
| M | T | W | T | F | S | S |
|---|---|---|---|---|---|---|
| | | | | | 1 | 2 |
| 3 | 4 | 5 | 6 | 7 | 8 | 9 |
| 10 | 11 | 12 | 13 | 14 | 15 | 16 |
| 17 | 18 | 19 | 20 | 21 | 22 | 23 |
| 24 | 25 | 26 | 27 | 28 | 29 | 30 |
| 31 | | | | | | |

# CALENDAR 2019

### JANUARY
| M | T | W | T | F | S | S |
|---|---|---|---|---|---|---|
| | 1 | 2 | 3 | 4 | 5 | 6 |
| 7 | 8 | 9 | 10 | 11 | 12 | 13 |
| 14 | 15 | 16 | 17 | 18 | 19 | 20 |
| 21 | 22 | 23 | 24 | 25 | 26 | 27 |
| 28 | 29 | 30 | 31 | | | |

### FEBRUARY
| M | T | W | T | F | S | S |
|---|---|---|---|---|---|---|
| | | | | 1 | 2 | 3 |
| 4 | 5 | 6 | 7 | 8 | 9 | 10 |
| 11 | 12 | 13 | 14 | 15 | 16 | 17 |
| 18 | 19 | 20 | 21 | 22 | 23 | 24 |
| 25 | 26 | 27 | 28 | | | |

### MARCH
| M | T | W | T | F | S | S |
|---|---|---|---|---|---|---|
| | | | | 1 | 2 | 3 |
| 4 | 5 | 6 | 7 | 8 | 9 | 10 |
| 11 | 12 | 13 | 14 | 15 | 16 | 17 |
| 18 | 19 | 20 | 21 | 22 | 23 | 24 |
| 25 | 26 | 27 | 28 | 29 | 30 | 31 |

### APRIL
| M | T | W | T | F | S | S |
|---|---|---|---|---|---|---|
| 1 | 2 | 3 | 4 | 5 | 6 | 7 |
| 8 | 9 | 10 | 11 | 12 | 13 | 14 |
| 15 | 16 | 17 | 18 | 19 | 20 | 21 |
| 22 | 23 | 24 | 25 | 26 | 27 | 28 |
| 29 | 30 | | | | | |

### MAY
| M | T | W | T | F | S | S |
|---|---|---|---|---|---|---|
| | | 1 | 2 | 3 | 4 | 5 |
| 6 | 7 | 8 | 9 | 10 | 11 | 12 |
| 13 | 14 | 15 | 16 | 17 | 18 | 19 |
| 20 | 21 | 22 | 23 | 24 | 25 | 26 |
| 27 | 28 | 29 | 30 | 31 | | |

### JUNE
| M | T | W | T | F | S | S |
|---|---|---|---|---|---|---|
| | | | | | 1 | 2 |
| 3 | 4 | 5 | 6 | 7 | 8 | 9 |
| 10 | 11 | 12 | 13 | 14 | 15 | 16 |
| 17 | 18 | 19 | 20 | 21 | 22 | 23 |
| 24 | 25 | 26 | 27 | 28 | 29 | 30 |

### JULY
| M | T | W | T | F | S | S |
|---|---|---|---|---|---|---|
| 1 | 2 | 3 | 4 | 5 | 6 | 7 |
| 8 | 9 | 10 | 11 | 12 | 13 | 14 |
| 15 | 16 | 17 | 18 | 19 | 20 | 21 |
| 22 | 23 | 24 | 25 | 26 | 27 | 28 |
| 29 | 30 | 31 | | | | |

### AUGUST
| M | T | W | T | F | S | S |
|---|---|---|---|---|---|---|
| | | | 1 | 2 | 3 | 4 |
| 5 | 6 | 7 | 8 | 9 | 10 | 11 |
| 12 | 13 | 14 | 15 | 16 | 17 | 18 |
| 19 | 20 | 21 | 22 | 23 | 24 | 25 |
| 26 | 27 | 28 | 29 | 30 | 31 | |

### SEPTEMBER
| M | T | W | T | F | S | S |
|---|---|---|---|---|---|---|
| | | | | | | 1 |
| 2 | 3 | 4 | 5 | 6 | 7 | 8 |
| 9 | 10 | 11 | 12 | 13 | 14 | 15 |
| 16 | 17 | 18 | 19 | 20 | 21 | 22 |
| 23 | 24 | 25 | 26 | 27 | 28 | 29 |
| 30 | | | | | | |

### OCTOBER
| M | T | W | T | F | S | S |
|---|---|---|---|---|---|---|
| | 1 | 2 | 3 | 4 | 5 | 6 |
| 7 | 8 | 9 | 10 | 11 | 12 | 13 |
| 14 | 15 | 16 | 17 | 18 | 19 | 20 |
| 21 | 22 | 23 | 24 | 25 | 26 | 27 |
| 28 | 29 | 30 | 31 | | | |

### NOVEMBER
| M | T | W | T | F | S | S |
|---|---|---|---|---|---|---|
| | | | | 1 | 2 | 3 |
| 4 | 5 | 6 | 7 | 8 | 9 | 10 |
| 11 | 12 | 13 | 14 | 15 | 16 | 17 |
| 18 | 19 | 20 | 21 | 22 | 23 | 24 |
| 25 | 26 | 27 | 28 | 29 | 30 | |

### DECEMBER
| M | T | W | T | F | S | S |
|---|---|---|---|---|---|---|
| | | | | | | 1 |
| 2 | 3 | 4 | 5 | 6 | 7 | 8 |
| 9 | 10 | 11 | 12 | 13 | 14 | 15 |
| 16 | 17 | 18 | 19 | 20 | 21 | 22 |
| 23 | 24 | 25 | 26 | 27 | 28 | 29 |
| 30 | 31 | | | | | |

# INTRODUCTION

Founded in 1753, the British Museum was the first national public museum in the world. From the outset it was a museum of the world, for the world, and this idea still lies at the heart of the Museum's mission today. The collection tells the stories of cultures across the world, from the dawn of human history, over two million years ago, to the present. Objects range from the earliest tools made by humans and treasures from the ancient world to more recent acquisitions from Africa, Oceania and the Americas, the Middle East, Asia and Europe, as well as the national collections of prints and drawings, and coins and medals.

In addition to work in London, the Museum takes part in an extensive programme of loans and tours, both across the UK and throughout the world. Today the Museum is the most popular visitor attraction in the United Kingdom, receiving nearly 6.9 million visitors from across the world last year.

This 2018 Diary is beautifully illustrated with objects from the collections of the British Museum. For more information on the British Museum and its collection, visit www.britishmuseum.org.

Bronze head from a statue of the emperor Hadrian, AD 117–138, from Roman London, British Museum 1848,1103.1

# January

---

**01** Monday

New Year's Day
Holiday, UK, Republic of Ireland, USA, Canada,
Australia and New Zealand

---

**02** Tuesday

Full moon
Holiday, Scotland and New Zealand

---

**03** Wednesday

---

**04** Thursday

---

**05** Friday

---

**06** Saturday

Epiphany

---

**07** Sunday

---

Painting of Viṣṇu as Kṛishṇa Govardhanadhara with attendants, Mughal style, late 17th century, Deccan, India, British Museum 1974,0617,0.2.65

# January

Last quarter

Monday 08

Tuesday 09

Wednesday 10

Thursday 11

Friday 12

Saturday 13

Sunday 14

Silk embroidery panel with flowers and ducks (detail), Tang dynasty, 9th–10th century, from Cave 17, Qian Fo Dong (Caves of the Thousand Buddhas), near Dunhuang, Gansu province, China, British Museum MAS.857

# January

---

**15** Monday                                    Holiday, USA (Martin Luther King Jnr Day)

---

**16** Tuesday

---

**17** Wednesday                                                          New moon

---

**18** Thursday

---

**19** Friday

---

**20** Saturday

---

**21** Sunday

---

Folding fan made of gold leaf on paper, made by Kano Tanshin Morimasa, Edo period, late 17th century, Japan, British Museum 1981,0303,0.3

# January

---

Monday **22**

---

Tuesday **23**

---

First quarter

Wednesday **24**

---

Thursday **25**

---

Holiday, Australia (Australia Day)

Friday **26**

---

Saturday **27**

---

Sunday **28**

---

*The Noble Game of the Swan* (detail), 1821, game-board, England, British Museum 1893,0331.123

# January / February

**29** Monday

---

**30** Tuesday

---

**31** Wednesday                                                            Full moon

---

**01** Thursday

---

**02** Friday

---

**03** Saturday

---

**04** Sunday

---

The Lewis Chessmen (three pieces), c.1150–75, walrus ivory, found in Uig, Isle of Lewis,
British Museum 1831,1101.123, 124 & 125

# February

Monday 05

Accession of Queen Elizabeth II
Holiday, New Zealand (Waitangi Day)

Tuesday 06

Last quarter

Wednesday 07

Thursday 08

Friday 09

Saturday 10

Sunday 11

Gold and silver ingot, spirals, loops and sheets, 18th Dynasty, 1352–1336 BC, el-Amarna, Egypt, British
Museum EA68503; Axes, daggers and spearheads, Early Bronze Age, 1700–1500 BC, Arreton Down,
British Museum 1856,0627.43-44, 1908,0514.1, 1985,0302.1, 1988,1202.1, SLAntiq.743-8, WG.2074-5

# February

**12** Monday

**13** Tuesday                                         Shrove Tuesday

**14** Wednesday                                        Valentine's Day
                                                       Ash Wednesday

**15** Thursday                                             New moon

**16** Friday                                        Chinese New Year

**17** Saturday

**18** Sunday

*Rustam and the dying Suhrab*, illustrated by Mu'in Musavvir, 1649, Iran (Isfahan),
British Museum 1922,0711,0.2

# February

Holiday, USA (Presidents' Day)                                              Monday 19

Tuesday 20

Wednesday 21

Thursday 22

First quarter                                                                Friday 23

Saturday 24

Sunday 25

Ornament from a throne in the shape of a winged bull with human torso and head, Urartian period, c.750–700 BC, from Toprakkale, Turkey, British Museum 1877,1218.12

# February / March

---

**26** Monday

---

**27** Tuesday

---

**28** Wednesday

---

**01** Thursday                                     St David's Day

---

**02** Friday                                          Full Moon

---

**03** Saturday

---

**04** Sunday

---

*The Great Renunciation* (detail), a painting on silk depicting the fourth major event in the life of the Buddha (Palsangdo), Choson dynasty, early 18th century, Korea, British Museum 1996,1003,0.2

Gold nose or ear-ring set with gems, Mughal dynasty, 18th–19th century, India, British Museum OA+.14177;
Inlaid disc brooch, Anglo-Saxon, late 6th or early 7th century, from Grave 8, Wingham, Kent, England,
British Museum 1879,0524.34; Vandal disc brooch, Late Antique period, 5th century, Annaba, Algeria, British
Museum 1865,0518.1; Miniature locket, c.1635–40, England, painted by David Des Granges, British Museum

# March

Monday 05

Tuesday 06

Wednesday 07

Thursday 08

Last quarter

Friday 09

Saturday 10

Mother's Day, UK and Republic of Ireland

Sunday 11

Waddesdon Bequest 168; Pendant locket in the form of a heart, silver filigree and painted enamel, France or Netherlands (?), 18th century, British Museum 1978,1002.1161; Carolingian brooch with Arabic-inscribed glass setting, 8th–9th century, Ballycottin Bog, Ballycotton, Republic of Ireland, British Museum 1875,1211.11

# March

---

**12** Monday                                              Commonwealth Day

---

**13** Tuesday

---

**14** Wednesday

---

**15** Thursday

---

**16** Friday

---

**17** Saturday                                                    New moon
                                                          St Patrick's Day

---

**18** Sunday

---

Woman's jacket decorated with shell beadwork (detail), c.1870–83, Lampung, Sumatra, Indonesia,
British Museum As,+.1917

# March

---

Holiday, Northern Ireland and Republic of Ireland (St Patrick's Day)

Monday 19

---

Vernal Equinox (Spring begins)

Tuesday 20

---

Wednesday 21

---

Thursday 22

---

Friday 23

---

First quarter

Saturday 24

---

Palm Sunday
British Summer Time begins

Sunday 25

---

Enamelled porcelain vase, reign of Kangxi, Qing dynasty, 1662–1722, China,
British Museum Franks.1596, donated by Sir Augustus Wollaston Franks

# March / April

**26** Monday

**27** Tuesday

**28** Wednesday

**29** Thursday

Maundy Thursday

**30** Friday

Good Friday
Holiday, UK, Canada, Australia and New Zealand

**31** Saturday

Full moon
Holiday, Australia (Easter Saturday)
First day of Passover (Pesach)

**01** Sunday

Easter Sunday

*The Holy Thorn Reliquary*, c.1400, Late Medieval, Paris, France, British Museum Waddesdon Bequest 67

Easter Monday
Holiday, UK (exc. Scotland), Republic of Ireland,
Australia and New Zealand

Monday **02**

Tuesday **03**

Wednesday **04**

Thursday **05**

Friday **06**

Saturday **07**

Last quarter

Sunday **08**

Mummy and coffin of Hor (detail), 22nd Dynasty, c.945–715 BC, Thebes, Egypt, British Museum EA6659;
Mummy and coffin of Hor, 22nd Dynasty, c.945–715 BC, Thebes, Egypt, British Museum EA6659; Mummy
of Hornedjitef (detail), Ptolemaic period, 332–31 BC, Asasif (Thebes), Egypt, British Museum EA6679

# April

**09** Monday

**10** Tuesday

**11** Wednesday

**12** Thursday

**13** Friday

**14** Saturday

**15** Sunday

Spring-driven clock, made by Thomas Starck, 1620, Augsburg, British Museum 1958,1006.2063

New moon

Monday 16

Tuesday 17

Wednesday 18

Thursday 19

Friday 20

Birthday of Queen Elizabeth II

Saturday 21

First quarter

Sunday 22

Ikat-dyed silk ceremonial headdress with gold songket decoration, late 19th to early 20th century, Palembang, Sumatra, Indonesia, British Museum As1957,05.13; Cotton cloth, part of a girl's dance costume, c.1900–50, Cachar, India, British Museum As1948,10.34.a, donated by Mrs Ursula Betts

# April

---

**23** Monday                                                St George's Day

---

**24** Tuesday

---

**25** Wednesday                    Holiday, Australia and New Zealand (Anzac Day)

---

**26** Thursday

---

**27** Friday

---

**28** Saturday

---

**29** Sunday

---

*Still-life with a vase of flowers* (detail), facsimile of a watercolour by Jan van Huysum of 1735, from 'Ectypa' of Ploos van Amstel, 1777 (published in 1821), The Netherlands, British Museum 1856,0712.111

Lustre-painted pottery jar, c.1001–25, Syria, British Museum 1970,1105.1; Chlorite bowl, Early Dynastic III period, c.2600–2400 BC, The Royal Cemetery, Ur, southern Iraq, British Museum 1928,1010.427; Porcelain meiping with 'fahua'-type decoration, Ming dynasty, c.1450–1505, Jingdezhen, China, British Museum Franks.67, donated by Sir Augustus Wollaston Franks; Delftware jug, c.1620, London, England, British Museum 1931,0317.1.CR; Stoneware *maebyong* vase,

Full moon

Monday **30**

Tuesday **01**

Wednesday **02**

Thursday **03**

Friday **04**

Saturday **05**

Sunday **06**

inlaid *punchong* ware, early Joseon dynasty, 15th century, Korea, British Museum 1936,1012.129; Painted jar, Samarran period, c.6500–6000 BC, Samarra, Mesopotamia, British Museum 1924,0416.7; Faience vase in the form of a winged Eros riding a goose, Hellenistic, 300–250 BC, probably made in Alexandria, Egypt, British Museum 1875,1110.2

# May

**07** Monday

Early Spring Bank Holiday, UK
Holiday, Republic of Ireland

**08** Tuesday

Last quarter

**09** Wednesday

**10** Thursday

Ascension Day

**11** Friday

**12** Saturday

**13** Sunday

Mother's Day, USA, Canada, Australia and New Zealand

Book of the Dead of Hunefer frame 5 (detail), papyrus, 19th Dynasty, c.1285 BC, Egypt,
British Museum EA9901,5

Monday 14

New moon

Tuesday 15

First day of Ramadân (subject to sighting of the moon)

Wednesday 16

Thursday 17

Friday 18

Saturday 19

Whit Sunday
Feast of Weeks (Shavuot)

Sunday 20

Broad beaded collar or *wesekh*, 11th Dynasty, c.2020 BC, Deir el-Bahri (Thebes), Egypt,
British Museum EA40928

# May

**21** Monday                                          Holiday, Canada (Victoria Day)

**22** Tuesday                                                          First quarter

**23** Wednesday

**24** Thursday

**25** Friday

**26** Saturday

**27** Sunday                                                          Trinity Sunday

Painted roundel on leather of a floral design, 19th century, made in Andhra Pradesh, Nirmal, India, British Museum 2008,3010.1, acquisition funded by the Brooke Sewell Permanent Fund

# May / June

---

Spring Bank Holiday, UK
Holiday, USA (Memorial Day)

Monday 28

---

Full moon

Tuesday 29

---

Wednesday 30

---

Corpus Christi

Thursday 31

---

Friday 01

---

Coronation Day

Saturday 02

---

Sunday 03

---

*Orientalisches (In the Oriental Style)*, 1938, woodcut print by Wassily Kandinsky, Germany,
British Museum 2004,0602.91

# June

**04** Monday

Holiday, Republic of Ireland
Holiday, New Zealand (The Queen's Birthday)

**05** Tuesday

**06** Wednesday

Last quarter

**07** Thursday

**08** Friday

**09** Saturday

The Queen's Official Birthday (subject to confirmation)

**10** Sunday

Mosaic pavement, Roman, Saint-Romain, 2nd century, France, British Museum 1913,1013.1

# June

---

Holiday, Australia (The Queen's Birthday)

Monday **11**

---

Tuesday **12**

---

New moon

Wednesday **13**

---

Thursday **14**

---

Eid al-Fitr (end of Ramadân)
(subject to sighting of the moon)

Friday **15**

---

Saturday **16**

---

Father's Day, UK, Republic of Ireland, USA and Canada

Sunday **17**

---

*L'Ecuyere (The circus performer)*, 1898, plate in L'Estampe Moderne, print made by Richard Ranft, France, British Museum 1899,0120.167

# June

18 Monday

19 Tuesday

20 Wednesday                                                First quarter

21 Thursday                              Summer Solstice (Summer begins)

22 Friday

23 Saturday

24 Sunday

Embroidered woman's overdress (detail), 19th century, Palestinian Authority (Ramallah),
British Museum As1967,02.15

# June / July

Monday 25

Tuesday 26

Wednesday 27

Full moon

Thursday 28

Friday 29

Saturday 30

Canada Day

Sunday 01

Lidded bowl (the 'Vaso Vescovali'), c.1200, Khurasan (possibly Herat), British Museum 1950,0725.1

# July

**02** Monday                                                    Holiday, Canada (Canada Day)

**03** Tuesday

**04** Wednesday                                          Holiday, USA (Independence Day)

**05** Thursday

**06** Friday                                                                          Last quarter

**07** Saturday

**08** Sunday

Stele with standing figure of Viṣṇu carved in buff-coloured sandstone, 10th century, India, British Museum 1872,0701.41, donated by Mr John Bridge and his nieces, Miss Fanny Bridge and Mrs Edgar Baker in 1872

# July

---

Monday **09**

---

Tuesday **10**

---

Wednesday **11**

---

Holiday, Northern Ireland (Battle of the Boyne)

Thursday **12**

---

New moon

Friday **13**

---

Saturday **14**

---

St Swithin's Day

Sunday **15**

---

*Under the Wave, off Kanagawa ('The Great Wave')* (detail), from the series *Thirty-six Views of Mt. Fuji,* c.1831, Katsushika Hokusai, Japan, colour woodblock print, British Museum 2008,3008.1.JA

# July

**16** Monday

---

**17** Tuesday

---

**18** Wednesday

---

**19** Thursday                                                    First quarter

---

**20** Friday

---

**21** Saturday

---

**22** Sunday

---

Drawing of a Campanian red-figured neck-amphora (BM 1814,0704.537), from the collection of Charles Townley, 1768–1805, British Museum 2010,5006.422

# July

Monday 23

Tuesday 24

Wednesday 25

Thursday 26

Full moon

Friday 27

Saturday 28

Sunday 29

Embroidered cotton prayer cloth with prayer stone (*mohr-e-namaz*) (detail), 20th century, made in
Afghanistan, found in Hazara District, Pakistan, British Museum As1973,10.1.a-b

# July / August

**30** Monday

**31** Tuesday

**01** Wednesday

**02** Thursday

**03** Friday

**04** Saturday                                    Last quarter

**05** Sunday

*Five senses* (detail), c.1595, after Hendrik Goltzius, print by Jan Saenredamprint, The Netherlands,
British Museum 1874,0711.1861

# August

Holiday, Scotland and Republic of Ireland

Monday 06

Tuesday 07

Wednesday 08

Thursday 09

Friday 10

New moon

Saturday 11

Sunday 12

Copper alloy brooch, 1100–500 BC, Iron Age, found in Hallstatt, Austria, British Museum 1939,0501.7

# August

**13** Monday

**14** Tuesday

**15** Wednesday

**16** Thursday

**17** Friday

**18** Saturday                                                                First quarter

**19** Sunday

*The Korsun Mother of God*, icon, 18th century, Russia, British Museum 1998,0605.1

# August

Monday 20

Tuesday 21

Wednesday 22

Thursday 23

Friday 24

Saturday 25

Full moon

Sunday 26

Tent-hanging (detail), 20th century, Afghanistan, British Museum As2002,03.26

# August / September

**27** Monday                                    Summer Bank Holiday, UK (exc. Scotland)

**28** Tuesday

**29** Wednesday

**30** Thursday

**31** Friday

**01** Saturday

**02** Sunday                                    Father's Day, Australia and New Zealand

Ceramic beehive-cover, 19th–20th century, Iran (Tehran or Tabriz), British Museum 1993,0722.13

# September

---

Last quarter
Holiday, USA (Labor Day)
Holiday, Canada (Labour Day)

Monday **03**

---

Tuesday **04**

---

Wednesday **05**

---

Thursday **06**

---

Friday **07**

---

Saturday **08**

---

New moon

Sunday **09**

---

Limewood mummy portrait of a woman, Roman Period, c.160–170, Rubaiyat, Egypt,
British Museum EA65346

# September

**10** Monday                                    Jewish New Year (Rosh Hashanah)

**11** Tuesday

**12** Wednesday                                                    Islamic New Year

**13** Thursday

**14** Friday

**15** Saturday

**16** Sunday                                                          First quarter

Silver groat coin of Henry VII (1485–1509), minted in London, British Museum E.4906; Gold sovereign coin of Henry VII, minted in London, 1504–09, British Museum 1866,0713.1; Gold aureus coin of Augustus, minted in Rome, AD 27, Britsh Museum 1897,0604.4; Gold aureus coin of Domitian with portrait

of Flavia Julia, minted in Rome, AD 88–89, British Museum 1864,1128.45; *The Arras medallion*, electrotype copy made by Etienne Bourgey of an original Roman medallion of Constantius I (293–306), British Museum B.11477 (both sides shown); Silver penny of Eric Bloodaxe, minted in York, 952–954, British Museum E.5081 (both sides shown)

# September

---

Monday **17**

---

Tuesday **18**

---

Day of Atonement (Yom Kippur)                    Wednesday **19**

---

Thursday **20**

---

Friday **21**

---

Saturday **22**

---

Autumnal Equinox (Autumn begins)                    Sunday **23**

---

Gilded cartonnage mummy-mask, Late Period to Roman Period, 664 BC–1st century AD, Egypt, British Museum EA29472

# September

**24** Monday          First day of Tabernacles (Succoth)

**25** Tuesday          Full moon

**26** Wednesday

**27** Thursday

**28** Friday

**29** Saturday          Michaelmas Day

**30** Sunday

Silk altar valance (detail), Tang Dynasty, 9th–10th century, from Cave 17, Qian Fo Dong (Caves of the Thousand Buddhas), near Dunhuang, Gansu province, China, British Museum MAS.855

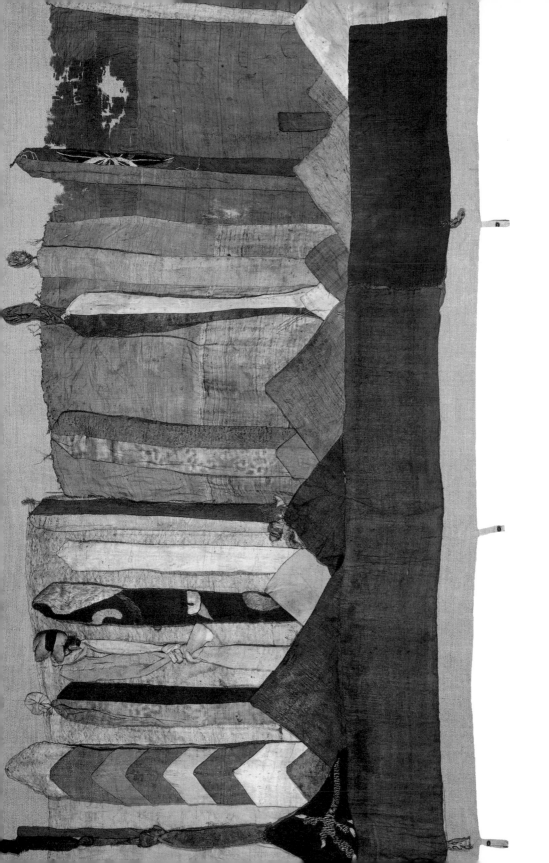

# October

---

Monday 01

---

Last quarter

Tuesday 02

---

Wednesday 03

---

Thursday 04

---

Friday 05

---

Saturday 06

---

Sunday 07

---

*Lily-of-the-valley and bugle*, c.1502–07, drawing from the circle of Albrecht Dürer, formerly attributed to Maria Sibylla Merian, Germany, British Museum 1895,0915.986

# October

**08** Monday

Holiday, USA (Columbus Day)
Holiday, Canada (Thanksgiving)

**09** Tuesday

New moon

**10** Wednesday

**11** Thursday

**12** Friday

**13** Saturday

**14** Sunday

Nuzi ware goblet decorated with flowers and plants, 1400–1300 BC, Late Bronze Age IIa, Tell Atchana, Turkey, Late Bronze Age IIa, British Museum 1938,0108.7

# October

---

Monday 15

---

First quarter

Tuesday 16

---

Wednesday 17

---

Thursday 18

---

Friday 19

---

Saturday 20

---

Sunday 21

---

A thang-kha of a Vasudhara maṇḍala (detail), 1504, Nepal, British Museum 1933,0722,0.1, donated by Sir Herbert Thompson

# October

**22** Monday            Holiday, New Zealand (Labour Day)

**23** Tuesday

**24** Wednesday            Full moon

**25** Thursday

**26** Friday

**27** Saturday

**28** Sunday            British Summer Time ends

Figure of Śiva Natarāja ('Lord of Cosmic Dance') in an oval mandorla edged with stylised flames, c.930–40 (?), Tamil Nadu, India, British Museum 1969,1216.1

# October / November

Holiday, Republic of Ireland

Monday 29

Tuesday 30

Last quarter
Halloween

Wednesday 31

All Saints' Day

Thursday 01

Friday 02

Saturday 03

Sunday 04

The Standard of Ur, c.2600–2400 BC, Early Dynastic III period, The Royal Cemetery, Ur, southern Iraq, British Museum 1928,1010.3

# November

---

**05** Monday

Guy Fawkes

---

**06** Tuesday

---

**07** Wednesday

New moon

---

**08** Thursday

---

**09** Friday

---

**10** Saturday

---

**11** Sunday

Remembrance Sunday

---

Panel from a mosaic floor showing edible fish from the Mediterranean area, c.100, Populonia, Tuscany, Italy, British Museum 1989,0322.1

# November

---

Holiday, USA (Veterans Day)
Holiday, Canada (Remembrance Day)

Monday **12**

---

Tuesday **13**

---

Wednesday **14**

---

First quarter

Thursday **15**

---

Friday **16**

---

Saturday **17**

---

Sunday **18**

---

*Kamisuki* ('*Combing the Hair*'), Hashiguchi Goyo, 1920, colour woodblock print, Japan, British Museum 1930,0910,0.1

# November

**19** Monday

**20** Tuesday

**21** Wednesday

**22** Thursday                                             Holiday, USA (Thanksgiving)

**23** Friday                                                            Full moon

**24** Saturday

**25** Sunday

Gold and enamel pendant reliquary, Byzantine, 13th century, Thessaloniki, Greece,
British Museum 1926,0409.1

# November / December

Monday 26

Tuesday 27

Wednesday 28

Thursday 29

Last quarter
St Andrew's Day

Friday 30

Saturday 01

First Sunday in Advent
Hannukah begins (at sunset)

Sunday 02

*Wrestlers*, c.1910–15, linocut print by Henri Gaudier-Brzeska, France, British Museum 1935,0226.1

# December

**03** Monday

**04** Tuesday

**05** Wednesday

**06** Thursday

**07** Friday                                                                                          New moon

**08** Saturday

**09** Sunday

Woman's short-sleeved jacket (detail), early 20th century, Palestinian Authority (Bethlehem or Beit Jala), British Museum As1966,01.3